SPIRIT & TRUTH

This book is dedicated to all of the truth seekers: Keep seeking God's truth and standing on His Word.

And to Kenny: For helping me to seek and stand firm through it all

-

For information contact:
SPIRIT & TRUTH
PO BOX 1737
MARTINSVILLE, IN 46151

spiritandtruthonline.org

Written and Dedicated by Kelli Young
Illustrations and Cover design by Brian P.
ISBN: 9781088216149

First Edition: December 2023

10 9 8 7 6 5 4 3 2 1

In a time long ago, in a place far away, there was a plan that was about to come into being. Through the battles of time, this plan was fought for. Through the errors of humans, this plan was redrafted. Through the silence of centuries, this plan was looked for.

This plan. This beautiful, perfect, incomprehensible, unimaginable, plan was woven through the threads of time. It was worked and weaved and sewn and stitched by the hands of God Almighty Himself. It was the perfect plan, by a perfect God, that had to be carried out perfectly, by people who were not perfect, no matter how hard they tried to be. It was a plan so big, so vast, so astounding, yet so simple it would only make sense to start with something so small, so tiny, so ordinary, yet so miraculous as the birth of a baby. This is where our story begins.

Around 3AD, a young Jewish girl named Mary lived in the city of Nazareth, in the land of Galilee. She lived a simple life, like the rest of her people.

She loved God and was watchful for the Messiah, the Promised Savior of her people, the Israelites. Mary would soon be married to a man named Joseph.

One day an angel named Gabriel, a messenger of God, was sent to Nazareth to speak to Mary.

"Greetings, favored one! The Lord is with you!" he said to Mary. "Do not be afraid, Mary, for you have found favor with God. You will have a baby in your womb and give birth to a son, and will call him Jesus. He will be great, and will be called the Son of the Most High, and the Lord God will give to him the throne of his father David and he will reign over the house of Jacob forever, and of his kingdom there will be no end."

Mary was confused and asked, "How will this be, since I am not yet married?"

"The Holy Spirit will come upon you, and the power of the Most High will overshadow you, and for that reason the holy one to be born will be called the Son of God. Your relative Elizabeth, she also has conceived a son in her old age, even though she was told she would never have a child; for nothing is impossible with God," replied Gabriel.

"I am the servant of the Lord. May it be done to me according to your word," said Mary. And then the angel Gabriel left.

In the days that followed, Mary hastily went to the hill country, to a city in the region of Judah, to the house where her pregnant cousin Elizabeth lived. As soon as Elizabeth heard Mary's greeting, the baby in her womb leaped, and holy spirit filled Elizabeth.

She told Mary, "Blessed are you among women, and blessed is the fruit of your womb. And how is this happening to me, that the mother of my Lord should come to me? When the voice of your greeting came into my ears, the baby in my womb leaped for joy. And blessed is she who believed, because all of the things spoken to you by the Lord will come true."

Mary, filled with joy and amazement about what was happening to her, cried out, "My soul magnifies the Lord, and my spirit rejoices in God my Savior because he has looked upon the low estate of his servant. From now on all generations will call me blessed, because the Mighty One has done great things for me, and holy is his name."

Mary stayed with Elizabeth, and they helped each other during their pregnancies, and rejoiced together and delighted in the fact that God had worked miracles for both of them! Now they would both have sons. After about 3 months, Mary returned to her house in Nazareth.

During that time, the ruler, Caesar Augustus, gave an order that everyone had to return to their own city to be registered for taxation.

Joseph and Mary went up from Nazareth into Judea, to Bethlehem, the city of David, to be registered—because they were both from the line of David. They set out with others who were traveling in the same direction. The journey was about 90 miles, and they walked along, stopping each night to make camp.

Almost a week later, they arrived in Bethlehem, and their relatives in the city took them in. Family was very important in Jewish culture, and everyone was overjoyed to welcome Joseph and his pregnant fiance into their town! Many other people were also arriving in Bethlehem for the registration, so kitchens were bustling with making extra food and the streets were noisy with extra people going to and fro.

While Mary and Joseph were staying in Bethlehem, the time came for the baby to be born. There was great excitement at the thought of a new baby. The men were escorted out of the house and the women bustled around as they prepared for the birth—stoking the fire to keep the room warm and getting water and cloth ready to clean the baby.

When the baby was born, there was great elation. It was a boy! Cheerful cries and shouts went out throughout the streets!

"It's a boy! God has blessed this family! The line of David continues!"

Mary wrapped the baby in swaddling clothes to keep him warm and dry, and placed him in a manger in the main room of the house, because the guest room was full of other relatives. The manger kept the new baby safe from the animals inside the house, who had been brought in for the night to be kept safe.

Part of God's great plan had already unfolded, but there was more to come. The beautiful baby boy had been born, the Savior of the world now lay in a manger in Bethlehem, and now God needed more people to spread the good news.

During this same warm night, there were shepherds in the fields keeping watch over their flocks. These shepherds were honest and trustworthy men who had been waiting all their lives for the Messiah to come. God chose these men to be the very first ones to tell people about Jesus, the Christ.

In the field where these shepherds watched their flocks, an angel of the Lord suddenly appeared before them, and the glory of the Lord shone around them.

The shepherds were frightened! What was this? What was happening?

"Do not be afraid! I come to you with good news that will bring great joy for all the people. A baby was born this day in the city of David— the Savior, who is the Messiah and Lord. And this will be the sign for you: you will find a baby wrapped in swaddling clothes and lying in a manger," the angel said to them.

Suddenly there was a crowd of many angels from God's heavenly army praising and saying, "Glory in the highest heavens to God, and on earth peace among people with whom he is well pleased."

Then, just as quickly as they had appeared, they were gone. The shepherds were amazed and went straight to Bethlehem to see the baby that the angels had told them about. They hurried into the town and easily found the house where a baby boy had been born, because of the celebration and joy that were still going on. They saw the baby lying in the manger and knew that what the angel had told them was true!

The Messiah had been born! The Savior was here! They were saved!

What joy! What great news! After all this time, Israel was saved!

The shepherds told everyone in town. They could not keep this news to themselves. They had to share it with everyone who would listen—about the field, the angels, the glory of God, the words that were spoken, the child in the manger. It was all just as God had said.

Everyone who listened to them was amazed at what they said. Could this be true? Had the Messiah been born here on this night?

It was true. And these are just a few of the amazing things that would happen because of this child.

Mary rested and looked over her new baby boy, Jesus. What a perfect child she had been given. What love she had for him already. What amazing things were already happening because he had been born. She took it all in and treasured it all in her heart.

God's plan had now come into being. God's son had been born.

SPIRIT & TRUTH
KiDS

We understand that the depictions of the birth of Jesus Christ in this book are unlike most records of the Christmas Story you see today.

If you would like to dive deeper into the accurate account of the Christmas Story, with plenty of biblical and extrabiblical evidence from the ancient Hebrew culture, you can visit:

https://spiritandtruthonline.org/retelling-the-christmas-story/

Or, for a video explaining the overview of what really happened surrounding the birth of Christ:

https://spiritandtruthonline.org/youtube/a-biblical-overview-of-the-true-christmas-story/

Printed in the USA
CPSIA information can be obtained
at www.ICGtesting.com
LVHW071251101123
763415LV00002B/2